GAMES FOR CHURCH GROUPS (PRIMARY)

Edited by
Mary Tucker

illustrated by
Janet Armbrust

W9-AGC-319

Cover by Ron Wheeler

Copyright © 1995 Shining Star
A publication of Silver Burdett Ginn Religion Division

ISBN No. 0-382-30651-1

Standardized Subject Code TA ac

Printing No. 987654321

Shining Star Publications
1204 Buchanan St., Box 399
Carthage, IL 62321

St. Louis de Montfort
1441 Hague Rd.
Fishers, IN 46038

The purchase of this book entitles the buyer to reproduce student activity pages for church and classroom use only. Not for resale. Any other use requires written permission from Shining Star Publications.

All rights reserved. Printed in the United States of America.

Unless otherwise indicated, the New International Version of the Bible was used in preparing the activities in this book.

TO THE TEACHER/PARENT

Children love to play games! But sometimes parents and teachers feel that games are just a way to "blow off steam" before or after a quiet time of learning. That needn't always be the case, however. Included in this book are various kinds of games that will allow children to learn important truths and concepts as they are playing and will help teachers provide fun ways to review and reinforce Bible lessons.

You may be surprised at how much a child will learn and remember from a game in which all his attention seems to be on running around in a circle or on beating the opposing team. Of course, in order for your children to benefit from the games in this book, or from any game, you must take time to plan carefully. Gathering children together before you have made all the necessary preparations for a game is a sure way to lose control and have discipline problems. Instead, choose the game at least an hour before you plan to use it, gather the materials needed, rearrange the room if necessary, and mark off the boundaries with tape. If you're playing outside, have specific boundaries and starting and ending lines in mind.

Another important step in your "game plan" is to think through the rules carefully, planning for every possible contingency. For example: Your children are playing tag and one child claims she has tagged another because she touched her hair! Does that count? Where does a child have to be tagged in order to be truly and properly tagged? What if your children are running the "Light as a Feather Relay" and one child uses his head to keep the feather from flying off his plate? Does that count? Make sure the rules are clear to everyone before the game begins.

Of course, one of the most important things about letting your children play games is to let them enjoy themselves. Be enthusiastic. (Don't keep pointing out things they shouldn't do; rather, encourage them to do their best!) Be sure to guide conversation whenever possible to help the children focus on the lesson or truth behind the game. This will be easy on the quiet games and table games. But even during the active games you should be able to interject a positive statement relating to the aim now and then.

Children's games are usually more fun when you have plenty of helpers to keep the children lined up and in the right places, to keep track of individual and team scores, and to cheer the children on. Teenagers make excellent, enthusiastic helpers, but parents and even grandparents will also add a special touch of fun to the proceedings.

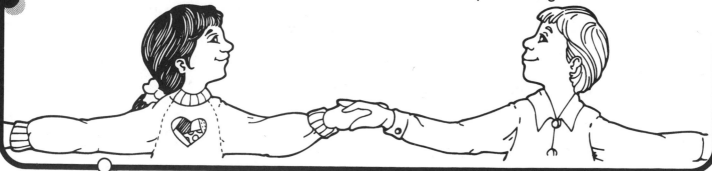

TABLE OF CONTENTS

Shining Star, Copyright © 1995   0-382-30651-1

Shining Star, Copyright © 1995
0-382-30651-1

ACTIVE GAMES

Shining Star, Copyright © 1995

0-382-30651-1

NOAH'S RAINSTORM

by Mary Tucker

TEACHING AIM: To reinforce the story of Noah and the Ark

MATERIALS NEEDED: Rainwear items (umbrella, hat, bag, rainscarf, boots)— one less item than the number of children playing, music cassette and cassette player (optional)

PREPARATION: Place the rainwear items in a pile in the center of the room.

PLAYING THE GAME: Have the children stand in a large circle around the pile of rainwear items. Play lively music (children's praise choruses would be nice). Children walk or skip around the circle. When the music stops, each child runs to the rainwear pile, grabs an item, and puts it on or holds it up if it cannot be worn. The child left with nothing to wear or hold up is out of the circle. Take one item off the rainwear pile and start the music again. Continue playing until only one child is left. Instead of playing music, you may prefer to play sounds of a rainstorm.

NOTE: When the rain sounds stop, the children grab rainwear items!

SHEEP, SHEEP, GOAT

by LaRayne Meyer

TEACHING AIM: To reinforce the story of the shepherd and his sheep

MATERIALS NEEDED: None

PREPARATION: Seat the children in a circle on the floor or ground.

PLAYING THE GAME: Choose a child to be the shepherd. The shepherd walks around the outside of the circle. He places his hand on the head of each child in the circle and says, "Sheep." When he places his hand on a child's head and says, "Goat," that child gets up and chases the shepherd around the circle. The shepherd must run around the circle and sit down in the goat's place before being tagged. If the shepherd is tagged, the goat sits back down and the shepherd goes around the circle until he chooses another goat. If the shepherd is not tagged, the goat becomes the shepherd.

Shining Star, Copyright © 1995

0-382-30651-1

THE PRODIGAL SON

by LaRayne Meyer

TEACHING AIM: To reinforce the story of the Prodigal Son

MATERIALS NEEDED: None

PREPARATION: Divide the children into two teams.

PLAYING THE GAME: The members of each team line up in a horizontal line, holding hands. The two teams should be facing each other with at least thirty feet between them. One team calls the name of a child from the opposing team, saying, "Prodigal Son (or Prodigal Child), don't you roam. (Meagan), won't you come home?" The child named runs toward the other team, trying to break through the line of linked hands. If she breaks through the line, the runner may return to her own team. If she is unable to break through the line, she becomes a member of the team who called her over. Teams take turns calling on opposing teammembers until time is called. The team with the most members wins.

Shining Star, Copyright © 1995

0-382-30651-1

NINETY-NINE SHEEP

by LaRayne Meyer

TEACHING AIM: To reinforce the story of the shepherd and his sheep

MATERIALS NEEDED: None

PREPARATION: Mark a spot to be home base.

PLAYING THE GAME: Choose a child to be the wolf. The rest of the children represent the ninety-nine sheep. The wolf hides his eyes at home base and counts to ninety-nine while the sheep hide. (You may want to set specific boundaries within which children may hide.) When the wolf is done counting, he calls out, "Howl, growl, hoo, hoo, I am hungry for mutton stew!" Then he starts searching for the lost sheep. If the wolf spots a sheep, he runs back to home base and calls out the name of the sheep: "(Eric) is my supper!" That sheep is then out of the game. If a sheep reaches home base when the wolf is not looking, she calls out, "This sheep is home free!" and is safe. The game ends when all the sheep have been found or have reached home base.

Shining Star, Copyright © 1995
0-382-30651-1

FOLLOW ME

by Connie Holman

TEACHING AIM: To help children consider how Satan wants to trick them into not following the Lord and to understand how they need to withstand his temptations

MATERIALS NEEDED: Stopwatch

PREPARATION: None

PLAYING THE GAME: Choose a child to be the leader and two or three to be "deceivers," facing the rest of the group. The leader makes a motion which the rest of the group imitates, changing to a different motion every ten or fifteen seconds. The "deceivers" try to gain followers by purposely doing incorrect motions. When a child imitates a "deceiver rather than the leader," he also becomes a "deceiver." The object is for the leader to continue his motions for one full minute with no one being tricked into following the "deceivers." After one minute, choose a new leader and new "deceivers" and continue the game.

NOTE: After the game, discuss children's feelings toward the "deceivers." Was it hard or easy to ignore them? Then talk about real-life situations and the difficulties in keeping our eyes on Jesus our leader instead of following Satan the deceiver.

ELIJAH AND THE RAVENS

by Mary Tucker

TEACHING AIM: To reinforce the story of Elijah and the ravens whom God used to feed him

MATERIALS NEEDED: A sheet of black construction paper for each pair of children

PREPARATION: Divide children into pairs or let them choose partners. Using masking tape (for indoors) or a rope (for outdoors), make two parallel lines about ten feet apart.

PLAYING THE GAME: Give each pair of children a piece of black construction paper and have them work together to fold the paper into a raven (like a paper airplane). When everyone's raven is done, line the children up in back of the lines with partners facing each other. When you give the signal to start, the children begin "flying" their ravens to their partners. If the raven is caught while still in the air, the pair gets a point. The receiving partner must not step across the line to catch the raven! As soon as one partner catches the raven, he flies it back to the other partner. At the end of a predetermined amount of time, the pair with the most points wins.

NOTE: With so much activity going on, you may want to appoint helpers to watch two or three pairs and keep track of their scores.

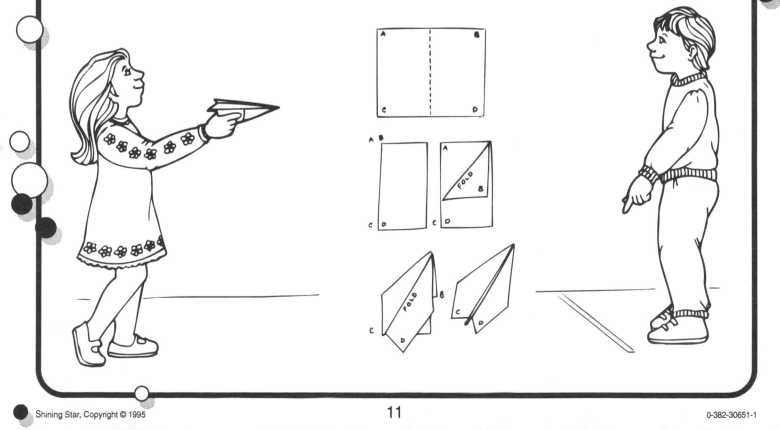

Shining Star, Copyright © 1995
0-382-30651-1

"LIGHT AS A FEATHER"

by Mary Tucker

TEACHING AIM: To reinforce the story of Creation and help children think about the special features God gave birds to help them fly

MATERIALS NEEDED: A large box or tub filled with feathers (ask parents for old feather pillows you can tear apart), two smaller boxes or tubs, two plastic or paper plates

PREPARATION: Place the large container of feathers at one end of the room. At the other end of the room, place the two smaller empty containers about six feel apart. Divide the children into two teams.

PLAYING THE GAME: Line the teams up on opposite sides of the room next to the empty containers. Give the first child on each team a plate. The child runs with the plate in one hand (the other hand must be behind the back or in a pocket) to the container of feathers, scoops up as many as possible on the plate, and quickly carries them back to empty them in the team's empty container. Of course, hurrying will cause most of the feathers to fly off the plate, but the child may not use his other hand to hold them down. The team with the most feathers in their container when time is called wins the game.

NOTE: This game may be played outside, but not on a breezy day!

Shining Star, Copyright © 1995

0-382-30651-1

CREATION HUNT

by Mary Tucker

TEACHING AIM: To reinforce the story of Creation and help children appreciate the world around them

MATERIALS NEEDED: A small paper bag for each individual or team

PREPARATION: Make a list of natural objects that can be found fairly easily in your neighborhood: yellow flower, round stone, clover, acorn, live ant, tree bark, bird feather, etc.

PLAYING THE GAME: Divide children into pairs or teams or let them play this game as individuals. Give each a small paper bag and a list of natural objects to be found. Set specific boundaries for the area to be searched. The first one to bring back all the objects on the list wins the game. If no one finds all the objects, end the hunt at a predetermined time, declaring the one with the most objects on the list the winner.

Shining Star, Copyright © 1995

0-382-30651-1

"I'M SPECIAL" TAG

by Mary Tucker

TEACHING AIM: To help children realize that God made each of us unique and different from others and to appreciate each person's uniqueness

MATERIALS NEEDED: None

PREPARATION: None

PLAYING THE GAME: Tell children to tag someone in the group who has black hair. After thirty seconds, mention another characteristic such as blue eyes. Continue changing the tagging instructions every thirty seconds so that the children are constantly trying to tag someone while trying to avoid being tagged themselves. When children are tagged, they are out of the game, but may get back in when the teacher mentions a new characteristic. (Make sure to mention physical characteristics shared by two or more children so one child is not chased by everyone else.)

NOTE: You may also want to mention characteristics such as first names, streets or towns where they live, and schools they attend.

Shining Star, Copyright © 1995

0-382-30651-1

ANIMAL SOUNDS

by Susan Addington

TEACHING AIM: To reinforce the stories of Creation and Noah and the Ark

MATERIALS NEEDED: Two dice, 3" x 5" cards containing pictures of animals with familiar sounds

PREPARATION: Glue pictures of animals on 3" x 5" cards. Make at least one for every child.

PLAYING THE GAME: Seat the children in two horizontal lines about a foot and a half apart, facing each other. Give each child an animal card. Give children a couple of minutes to practice making the sounds of the animals pictured on their cards and listening to each other. The first player on each team rolls a die. If the numbers on the dice are the same, each child tries to be the first to make the sound of the other child's animal. The one who is first earns a point for his team. If the numbers on the two dice do not match, the dice are passed to the next two children in line to continue the game. At the end of a predetermined time, the team with the most points wins.

NOTE: When the children are done playing this game, mount the animal cards on a bulletin board with the caption "God's world is full of creatures of all shapes and sounds!"

Shining Star, Copyright © 1995

0-382-30651-1

BEANO BOD! EVEN OR ODD?

by Susan Addington

TEACHING AIM: To reinforce the parable of the seeds and the sower

MATERIALS NEEDED: A bag of dried beans, small bags or margarine tubs

PREPARATION: Put ten dried beans in a small bag or a margarine tub for each child.

PLAYING THE GAME: Each child walks around the room holding a container of beans in one hand and an even or odd number of beans hidden in the other hand. The child asks another child, "Beano Bod! Even or Odd?" If the child asked guesses correctly, the first child opens his hand and gives the guesser the beans in it. If the guess is incorrect, the guesser forfeits that same number of beans to the first child. Children continue to circulate, changing the number of beans in their hands, asking others to guess even or odd. If a child runs out of beans before time is up, he is out of the game and must sit down. When time is called, the child with the most beans is the winner.

NOTE: This game may also be played to reinforce the story of God choosing David in 1 Samuel 16. Emphasize to children that we only see the outside of people, but God sees inside each of us. He knows our hearts.

JOSEPH'S ROBE RELAY

by Susan Addington

TEACHING AIM: To reinforce the story of Joseph and his coat of many colors

MATERIALS NEEDED: A large, old shirt for each team

PREPARATION: None

PLAYING THE GAME: Divide the children into two teams and give each team a shirt. The first person on each team puts on the shirt (without buttoning it). Then she holds the hand of a teammember. The rest of the team tries to take the shirt off the first child and put it on the second child without breaking the linked hands. (This can only be done by turning the shirt inside out as it goes over the first child's head.) The second child lets go of the first child's hand and holds hands with another one and the team repeats the procedure, moving the shirt from one child to another. Play continues until all the children on the team have worn the shirt. The team that finishes first wins the race.

NOTE: This game is best played with at least four players on each team.

Shining Star, Copyright © 1995
0-382-30651-1

MISSIONARY RACE AROUND THE WORLD

by Susan Addington

TEACHING AIM: To reinforce lessons on world missions and discussions on taking God's Word around the world

MATERIALS NEEDED: Two playground balls of equal size

PREPARATION: None

PLAYING THE GAME: Divide the children into two teams and have each team stand in a large circle. Have each team select a captain. Give each captain a ball. When you give the signal, each captain quickly passes the ball to the child on his right. Children continue passing the ball from hand to hand around the circle (the world). When the ball gets to the captain again, he calls out "once" and keeps it going for the second and third rounds. If the ball is dropped, it must be given to the captain to start the round again. The first team to get the ball all the way around the world (the circle) three times wins the game.

NOTE: You may prefer to have each team sit or kneel in a circle to play the game.

Shining Star, Copyright © 1995

0-382-30651-1

RAINY DAY SCAVENGER HUNT

by Susan Addington

TEACHING AIM: To help children think about and be thankful for what God has given them

MATERIALS NEEDED: Old magazines, pencil, and list of items for each child or team

PREPARATION: List ten or more things God gives us that may be illustrated in magazines (food, clothes, house, plants, pets, etc.). Copy the list for each child or team.

PLAYING THE GAME: Place a pile of old magazines in the center of the room. Give each child or team a list of things to hunt for and a pencil. When you say go, children take magazines and begin looking through them for the things on the list. They must tear out the pictures and check off the items as they find them. After a predetermined time, the team or individual with the most pictures on the list wins the game.

NOTE: Instead of designating a list of items, specify a certain topic and the number of pictures to be found. For example: Find ten things you eat with your fingers or find five different plants.

You may want to give younger children a list using pictures instead of words.

Shining Star, Copyright © 1995

0-382-30651-1

RECYCLING RELAYS

by Susan Addington

TEACHING AIM: To reinforce lessons on taking care of God's world or to spark discussion on Jesus' power to change our old habits into new actions or attitudes

MATERIALS NEEDED: Empty soda pop cans or plastic liter bottles, margarine or whipped topping tubs, newspapers

PREPARATION: Mark off start and finish lines with masking tape (if you're playing indoors) or rope (if you're playing outdoors). Divide the children into teams.

PLAYING THE GAMES:

RELAY 1: Give the first child on each team a soda pop can or plastic liter bottle. Each child must crawl on hands and knees, rolling the can or bottle with the head to a predetermined mark, then pick it up and run back to the starting line to give it to the next child on the team. The first team done wins.

RELAY 2: Give the first child on each team a margarine or whipped topping tub. Each child must walk as quickly as possible to a predetermined mark with the tub balanced on the head. If the tub falls off, it must be picked up and placed back on the head before the child may continue walking. After reaching the mark, the child may hold the tub on his head as he runs back to the starting line to give the tub to the next child. The first team done wins.

RELAY 3: Line up the teams behind piles of newspaper. The first child on each team makes a newspaper hat, sticks it on her head, and races to a predetermined mark, then back to the starting line. If the hat falls off, she must pick it up and put it back on her head before continuing. The second child in line must make his own paper hat from another newspaper before continuing the race. (To save time, you may want to let the second child make his hat while the first one is running.)

RELAY 4: Give the first child on each team a wadded-up newspaper sheet. He must hold the wad of paper under his chin while running to a predetermined mark and back to the next child in line. If the wad of paper is dropped, it must be picked up and put back under the chin before the child may continue running. The first team done wins.

HUMILITY BEANBAG TOSS

by Tamara Miller

TEACHING AIM: To help children learn the biblical teaching on humility and to understand what it means in their everyday lives

MATERIALS NEEDED: Question list (page 22), large piece of poster board, marker, beanbag, HUMILITY letter cards (optional)

PREPARATION: Use a marker to divide the poster board into nine even squares. Letter each square as shown below. Place the gameboard on the floor. You may also want to print the letters on index cards so you can keep track of the score by giving the correct letter card to the team that earns it. (Make a set of letter cards for each team.)

PLAYING THE GAME: Divide the children into teams, lining them up about eight feet from the gameboard. The first player on a team tosses the beanbag at the gameboard. If the beanbag lands on a letter, the child answers a question from the question list. If the answer is correct, the child's team keeps the letter. If the beanbag lands on the FREE square, the child may choose any letter on the gameboard. If he answer the question correctly, his team keeps the letter. If the beanbag misses the gameboard or falls on a letter the team already has, he does not get to answer a question, and it is the next team's turn. The first team to get all the letters to spell HUMILITY wins the game.

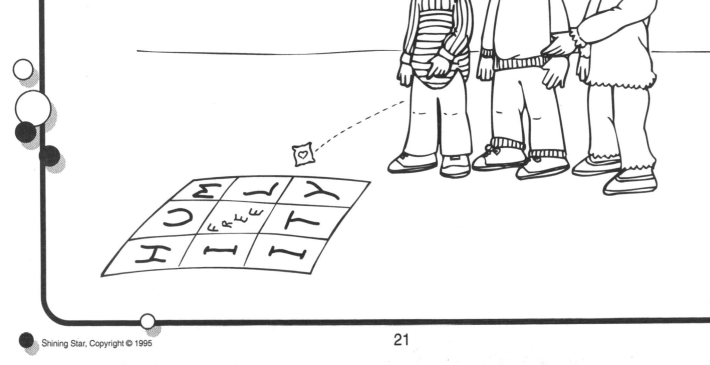

HUMILITY QUESTIONS:

1. Listen to Philippians 2:3. (Read it aloud.) Explain what HUMILITY means.
2. What is the opposite of being humble?
3. What is another word to describe someone who is humble?
4. Tell of a time when someone you know showed humility.
5. Tell of a time when Jesus showed humility.
6. Is it easy to be humble? Why or why not?
7. Listen to Proverbs 16:5. (Read it aloud.) How does God feel about people who are proud and arrogant?
8. Listen to James 4:6. (Read it aloud.) What does God give to the humble?
9. Listen to Philippians 2:4. (Read it aloud.) How can we show humility?
10. Listen to 1 Corinthians 13:4. How does true love act?
11. Tell of a time when someone you know acted with pride and arrogance.
12. How does it make you feel when you are around someone who is constantly bragging?
13. Listen to Romans 12:16. (Read it aloud.) What does God want us to do?
14. Listen to Proverbs 18:12. (Read it aloud.) What is the result of pride?
15. Listen to Proverbs 18:12. (Read it aloud.) What is the result of humility?
16. What can you do this week to show humility?
17. Listen to Colossians 3:23. (Read it aloud.) Is it wrong to try to do your best and be happy about your abilities?
18. How do you think God feels when we are proud and arrogant?
19. What does it mean to be a good winner?
20. Listen to Proverbs 27:2. (Read it aloud.) What does this verse teach us about bragging?
21. Listen to Matthew 23:11. (Read it aloud.) What did Jesus teach about being great?
22. Listen to Matthew 11:29. (Read it aloud.) Describe Jesus according to this verse.
23. Listen to Proverbs 8:13. (Read it aloud.) We should love God. What should we hate?
24. Listen to Colossians 3:12. (Read it aloud.) What kind of "clothes" should we wear?

WATCH OUT FOR LIES

by Tamara Miller

TEACHING AIM: To help children think about dishonesty and learn to recognize some lies that exist in our world today

MATERIALS NEEDED: Sheets of colored construction paper: 2 orange, 9 blue, 3 red, 3 white, 3 green, and 3 yellow; "Watch Out for Lies" questions (page 24) on individual red cards; Questions (page 24) on white cards; "What Would You Do?" questions (page 25) on green cards.

PREPARATION: Obtain a spinner or a die. Make a path on the floor, using sheets of colored construction paper. The path color sequence should be blue, green, red, blue, yellow, white and blue. Repeat this sequence three times. Each color should stand for a different instruction as follows:

ORANGE–"Start" and "Finish" (Place one at the beginning and one at the end of the path.)

BLUE–Children remain on these places until the next turn.

RED–When a child lands on one of these squares, he draws a "Watch Out for Lies" card. The leader reads the card aloud and leads a group discussion. Then the child goes back two squares and remains there until the next turn.

WHITE–Each child draws a question card when he lands on one of these squares, answers the question, and remains here until the next turn. (You may want to let children look up the Bible verses to find the answers.)

GREEN–When a child lands on a square of this color, he draws a "What Would You Do?" card and chooses an appropriate action as an answer. Then he remains on the square until the next turn.

YELLOW–Children who land on these squares may go ahead two spaces and remain there until the next turn.

PLAYING THE GAME: The first child rolls a die or spins a spinner to determine how many squares to walk over. He follows the instructions according to the color of the square on which he lands. The rest of the children take turns doing likewise. The first child to reach "Finish" wins the game.

NOTE: Instead of having a large path on which the children walk, you may want to make a smaller path on the table and use buttons for children to move from square to square.

Shining Star, Copyright © 1995

0-382-30651-1

"WATCH OUT FOR LIES" QUESTIONS (Type on individual red cards.)

1. Only beautiful people are worth anything in this world."
What does God's Word say? (1 Samuel 16:7; John 3:16; Romans 2:11; 15:7)
2. Everybody uses bad words or tells dirty jokes sometimes, so it's OK. And God understands if you have to tell a little lie now and then."
What does God's Word say? (Ephesians 4:29; 5:4; Colossians 3:9)
3. Nobody has the right to tell me what to do or how to live my life!"
What does God's Word say? (Romans 13:1; Ephesians 6:1; Titus 3:1; 1 Peter 2:13-14)
4. Every living thing began as a result of chance. What exists today evolved over billions of years."
What does God's Word say? (Genesis 1–2; John 1:3)
5. You can't be happy unless you have lots of money, a nice car, stylish clothes, a TV, a VCR, and lots of other things."
What does God's Word say? (Matthew 6:19-21; 6:24; Luke 12:15)
6. Don't let anybody get by with doing anything against you. Get even!" What does God's Word say? (Luke 6:35-36; Romans 12:17-21; 14:19)
7. We should pray for good people. Bad people don't deserve our prayers."
What does God's Word say? (Matthew 5:43-45; Luke 6:27-28)
8. Take care of yourself and don't worry about anyone else."
What does God's Word say? (Philippians 2:3-5a; James 1:27a)

QUESTIONS (Type on individual white cards.)

1. Who told the first lie? (Genesis 3:4)
2. Why did Satan lie to Eve about God?
3. What is impossible for God to do? (Hebrews 6:18)
4. Who said, "I am the way, the truth, and the life"? (John 14:6)
5. Who is called the "father of lies"? (John 8:44)
6. Where can we find the truth? (Psalm 119:160; John 17:17)
7. Why does God want us to tell the truth?
8. Whom can you fool by being dishonest?
9. Who always knows if we are being honest or dishonest?
10. What are some reasons that people tell lies?
11. What can happen if someone gets caught in a lie?
12. How is it possible to tell lies with your actions?

"WHAT WOULD YOU DO?" QUESTIONS (Type on individual green cards.)

1. While flipping through a book in the library, Susan accidentally ripped a page. What should she do?

2. Chris opened his car door and banged the side of another car in a crowded parking lot. It made a dent in the other car. What should he do?

3. John could not remember the capital of Rhode Island for a social studies test. Mark left a map on the floor next to his desk. What should John do?

4. Katie agreed to take care of Mrs. Wood's pets while she was out of town. She was paid in advance. Now Katie has lots of homework and doesn't feel she has time to do the work. What should she do?

5. Jack was playing with his BB gun and accidentally shot a hole in his neighbor's garage window. No one saw him do it. What should Jack do?

6. Harriet found a wallet with $20 in it in the school cafeteria. What should she do?

7. While playing at a friend's house, Julie accidentally broke a tomato plant in the back yard. She could blame it on the dog. What should Julie do?

8. When it was time to turn in his spelling homework, Frank realized he had forgotten to do it! What should he do?

9. Kelly's mom told her she couldn't have any candy because she hadn't eaten her supper. At a friend's house that evening, Kelly's friend offered her a candy bar. What should Kelly do?

10. David made a book report after just skimming the book. The last question on the report was, "Did you read the whole book?" What should David do?

11. Craig found a box of baseball cards on the playground. What should he do?

12. The Brown family went to a restaurant where kids under six eat free. The waitress asked seven-year-old Nancy what she wanted from the free children's menu. What should Nancy do?

13. Meagan hates to brush her teeth. She brushes at bedtime because her mother makes her. The dentist asked Meagan at her last checkup if she brushes three times a day. What should she do?

14. Dad told Donna he would pay her $5 to weed the flower beds. Two of Donna's friends came over and helped her. Dad was so impressed with her fast work, he gave her a bonus! What should Donna do?

15. When Pam and Tracy were shopping, Tracy saw a sweater she wanted. She took the $35 sweater into the dressing room with a $20 shirt and switched the price tags. What should Pam do?

QUIET GAMES

Shining Star, Copyright © 1995

0-382-30651-1

I WENT TO BETHLEHEM

by LaRayne Meyer

TEACHING AIM: To help children think about Jesus' birth in Bethlehem

MATERIALS NEEDED: None

PREPARATION: Place chairs in a row or a circle.

PLAYING THE GAME: The first child begins the game by saying, "I went to Bethlehem to visit Jesus and took a (an)_____," naming an item that begins with the letter A (apple, aardvark, ark, etc.). The second child says the same statement, repeating the "A" item mentioned by the first student and adding another item, this time beginning with the letter B (ball, Bible, etc.). The game continues with each child repeating the items already mentioned and adding another item beginning with the next letter of the alphabet. If a child cannot remember all the items mentioned or cannot name a new item, she is out of the game. The game continues until all the letters of the alphabet have been used or until only one child is left.

NOTE: This game may also be played with numbers: "I went to Bethlehem to visit Jesus and took 1 sheep, 2 books, 3 stars, 4 cakes, etc."

Shining Star, Copyright © 1995

0-382-30651-1

BOOKS OF THE BIBLE

by Rosa Brinkman

TEACHING AIM: To help children learn the books of the Bible

MATERIALS NEEDED: Two empty (clean) medium sized cans (16-ounce or larger), construction paper, glue, eleven 4" x 6" index cards, marker, scissors

PREPARATION: Cover the two cans with construction paper, glue it on, and print "Old Testament" on one and "New Testament" on the other. Cut each index card into six equal strips and print a book of the Bible on each strip.

PLAYING THE GAME: Place the books of the Bible strips on the table in scrambled order. Let children take turns picking up the strips and deciding whether to put them in the Old Testament or New Testament can. (You may want to provide an answer sheet so the children can check their work.)

NOTE: If older children are playing this game, you may want to use several cans to divide the books into divisions: History, Law, Poetry, etc.

Shining Star, Copyright © 1995

0-382-30651-1

BIBLE JEOPARDY

by Rosa Brinkman

TEACHING AIM: To help students learn or review important Bible verses and information

MATERIALS NEEDED: Poster board, 3" x 5" index cards, marker, Bibles (optional)

PREPARATION: Print across the top of the poster board "BIBLE JEOPARDY." Fold the index cards in half and write a Bible question on the inside of each card. On the outside front half of the card, print a number to show how many points the question is worth. Glue the cards to the poster board with the numbers facing out. You may want to prepare an answer page to check children's answers.

PLAYING THE GAME: Divide the children into teams. The first student on one team selects a number from the board, reads the question aloud on the inside of the card, and answers it. If the answer is correct, the child's team receives that number of points. The teams take turns choosing and answering questions until one team has a predetermined number of points or until all the questions have been answered. The team with the highest score wins.

NOTE: You may want to let children use their Bibles to find the answers to the questions. If so, make sure you list a Bible reference on each question card.

Shining Star, Copyright © 1995

0-382-30651-1

DAYS OF CREATION

by Rosa Brinkman

TEACHING AIM: To help children learn and review the Bible story of Creation, emphasizing what God created each day

MATERIALS NEEDED: Six 8½" x 11" sheets of paper; drawings or magazine pictures of light and darkness, sea and sky, trees and flowers, sun and moon, birds and fish, animals and man; glue; clear tape; construction paper; scissors

PREPARATION: Tape the six sheets of paper together to make a large gameboard divided into six parts. Glue the pictures on the gameboard as shown below. Draw large numbers 1–6 on construction paper and cut them out.

PLAYING THE GAME: Children take turns guessing on which day of Creation God made each item pictured. When a child guesses correctly, he may place the correct number on the things created that day.

NOTE: To help the children make correct guesses, read the Creation story aloud from Genesis 1.

Shining Star, Copyright © 1995

0-382-30651-1

THINGS WE LOVE

by Connie Holman

TEACHING AIM: To help children think about love and what it really means

MATERIALS NEEDED: Paper hearts (made from the pattern below), clear tape

PREPARATION: On paper hearts print things we often say we love: food, school subject, drink, sport, Bible character, ice cream, famous person, TV show, car. Tape these under the children's chairs before they arrive.

PLAYING THE GAME: Without letting anyone else see, each child finds and reads the paper heart under his chair, then thinks of one item in that category that he "loves." Children take turns saying what they love. The rest of the group tries to guess the categories. After everyone has had a turn or two, lead a discussion on what love really is, based on 1 Corinthians 13 or 1 John 4:7-12.

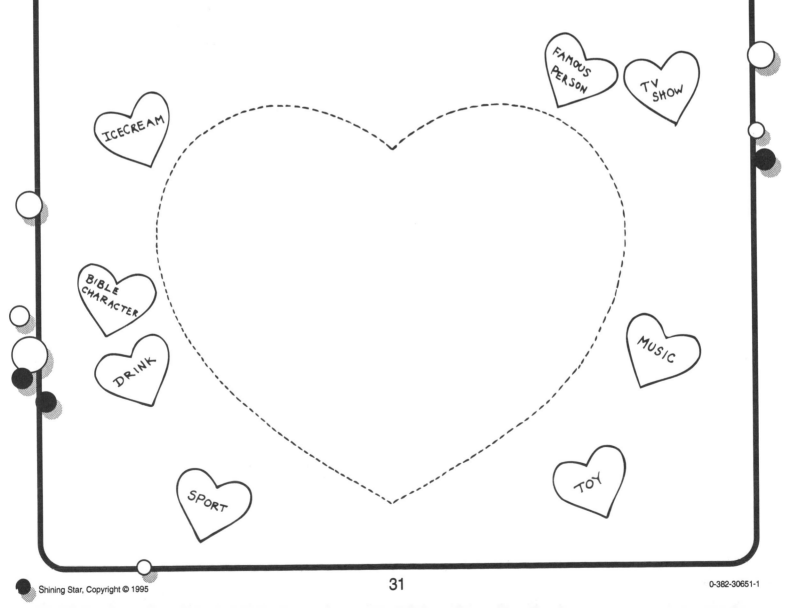

Shining Star, Copyright © 1995

0-382-30651-1

HOUSEBUILDERS

by Susan Addington

TEACHING AIM: To reinforce Bible stories about "building" such as the houses on the rock and sand, Jesus preparing a place for us in heaven, building loving homes

MATERIALS NEEDED: Pencil and paper and a die for each child or team

PREPARATION: Place the simple diagram of a house, shown below, on a wall or bulletin board.

PLAYING THE GAME: Each child or team rolls the die to determine what part of the house may be drawn according to the diagram. If a child throws a 1, he may draw one wall. (He will need three rolls of 1 to complete the walls.) If he throws a 2, he may draw half of the roof. Throwing a 3 lets him draw the front door; a 4 lets him draw one window; a 5 lets him draw the chimney; a 6 lets him draw the door knob on the door. The three walls must be finished before the rest of the house may be built, and the roof must be finished before the chimney is added. Otherwise, the parts of the house may be built in any order. The first person or team to complete the house wins the game.

NOTE: To make this game more challenging, have children use toothpicks to "build" their houses.

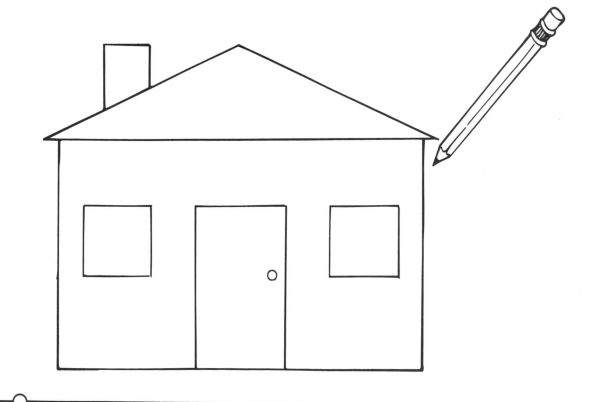

Shining Star, Copyright © 1995

0-382-30651-1

by Mary Tucker

TEACHING AIM: To help children think about the importance of Christlike character in everyday life

MATERIALS NEEDED: None

PREPARATION: Print on the chalkboard the character trait you want to emphasize (faith, courage, helpfulness, etc.).

PLAYING THE GAME: Seat children in a circle or around a table. Begin an imaginary story about a boy or girl the same age as most of your children. Create a situation; then choose a child to carry on the story, using her imagination to involve the person in the story in an action that reflects the character trait you're emphasizing. Let the child tell part of the story; then choose another child to add to it. Continue until all the children have had an opportunity to make up part of the story. (Example: Once there was a boy named Eric. His next door neighbor, Mrs. Olson, was an older woman who loved to work in her garden, but sometimes she wasn't able to kneel down to pull the weeks. (First child continues) Eric often went over and pulled weeds for Mrs. Olson. He always waited until he saw her in the garden because he didn't want to accidentally pull a healthy plant. (Second child continues) Eric sometimes watched his little sister while his mom fixed dinner. He pulled her in his wagon and showed her how to play catch with the ball.

MYSTERY ANIMAL

by Mary Tucker

TEACHING AIM: To reinforce the story of Creation and help children consider the amazing animals God made

MATERIALS NEEDED: None

PREPARATION: You may want to compile a list of animals beforehand and keep it handy in case some children need help coming up with ideas.

PLAYING THE GAME: Each child thinks of an animal. Choose one child to go first. He gives one hint to help the other children guess what animal he is. (Example: I'm very slow.) Children take turns asking questions which can only be answered with yes or no. (Example: Do you have a shell on your back?) After everyone has asked a question, if no one has guessed correctly, the child may "act out" how the animal moves. Keep this game quiet by making the children take turns, even to guess the identity of the animal.

Shining Star, Copyright © 1995

0-382-30651-1

JESUS IS...

by Mary Tucker

TEACHING AIM: To help children think about who Jesus is and how He may be described

MATERIALS NEEDED: None

PREPARATION: Print on the chalkboard "Jesus is . . .

PLAYING THE GAME: Seat children in a circle. The teacher begins the game by completing the statement on the board with a word that begins with the first letter of her own name. (Example: Teacher Mary says, "Jesus is my master.") The first child in the circle does the same, using the first letter of his first name. Continue around the circle this way. The second time around the circle, each child uses the first letter of his last name.

NOTE: To make this game more challenging, have each child repeat the words already given by the other children before he says his own. (Example: Chris says, "Jesus is my master, holy, loving, and caring."

Shining Star, Copyright © 1995

0-382-30651-1

WHICH DISCIPLE?

by Mary Tucker

TEACHING AIM: To help children learn or review the names of Jesus' twelve disciples

MATERIALS NEEDED: Disciples' names on slips of paper

PREPARATION: Arrange children's chairs in a large circle.

PLAYING THE GAME: Have the children sit in a circle. Choose one child to be "it" and to leave the room while you assign a disciple's name to each child. Give each a slip of paper with the name on it so it isn't forgotten. Call "it" back into the room. He walks around the inside of the circle saying, "Jesus had twelve disciples, and one of them was named _____." As he says the name of a disciple, "it" stops and kneels down in front of a child. If his guess is correct, that child becomes "it," and the game starts over with children being assigned names again. If "it" guesses incorrectly, he walks around the circle again and repeats the process until he makes a correct guess.

NOTE: This game may also be played using the names of Jacob's sons (the twelve tribes of Israel).

Shining Star, Copyright © 1995

0-382-30651-1

TABLE
GAMES

Shining Star, Copyright © 1995

0-382-30651-1

LEARNING PATIENCE

by Tamara Miller

TEACHING AIM: To help children learn about patience, what it is and how important it is in the Christian's life

MATERIALS NEEDED: Copy of the gameboard (page 39); the questions below, Scripture Check (page 40), and Application (page 41) cut apart and put in a separate box for each category, markers (buttons or other small objects), a spinner or die, crayons or markers, clear adhesive plastic

PREPARATION: Color the gameboard and cover it with clear adhesive plastic. (You may want to enlarge the gameboard to make it easier for several children to play.)

PLAYING THE GAME: Children place their markers on START. The first child rolls the die or spins the spinner to determine how many spaces to move his marker. He may move in any direction. When he lands on a space with a title on it, he draws a slip of paper from the appropriate box, and reads it. If a question is involved, he must answer it. If he draws a Scripture Check, he reads a Bible verse and answers a question. The rest of the children follow the same procedure. The first child to reach FINISH wins the game.

NOTE: Instead of having the children read the questions and statements for themselves, you may prefer to have the leader read the questions, Scripture Check, and application from separate lists.

QUESTIONS:

1. What does it mean to be patient?
2. Give an example of patience during pain or trouble.
3. What is one thing you must wait for patiently?
4. How is waiting patiently different from just waiting?
5. What does it mean to be impatient?
6. When do you need patience in school?
7. When do adults need patience?
8. What is perseverance?
9. Can a "hot-head" or quick-tempered person learn to be patient?
10. What are some ways you can ask someone to be patient?
11. When do you need patience at home?
12. When do people have to be patient with you?
13. What happens when people become impatient with one another?
14. Why does God want us to be patient?

Shining Star, Copyright © 1995

0-382-30651-1

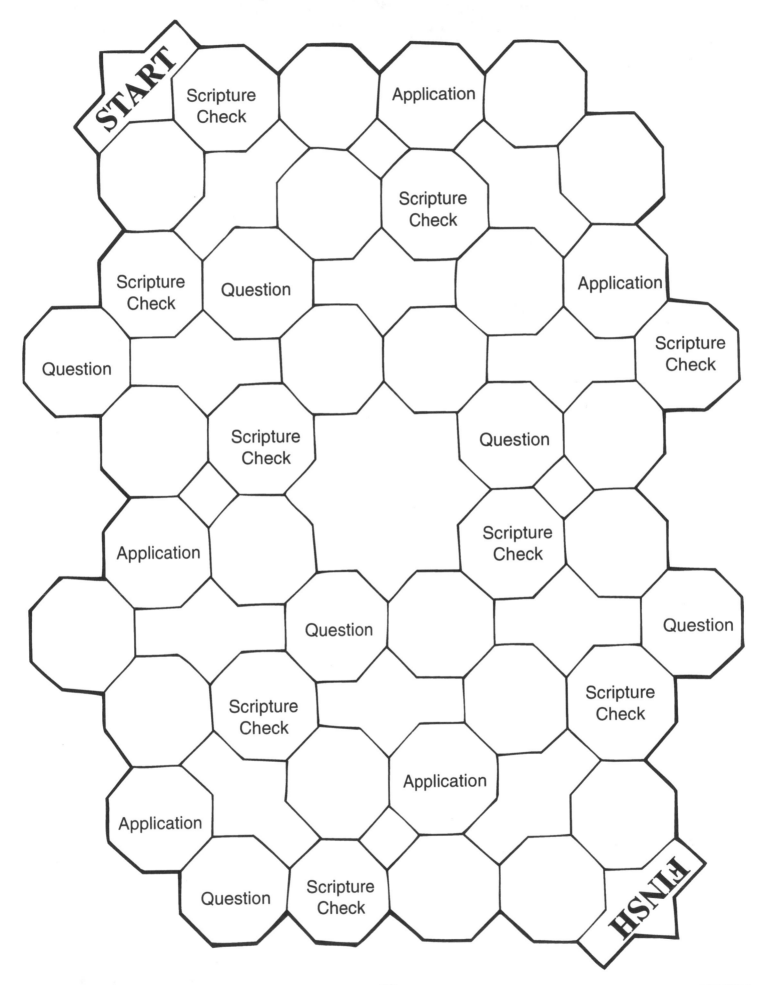

Shining Star, Copyright © 1995

0-382-30651-1

SCRIPTURE CHECK

Proverbs 14:29
What does Solomon say about a patient man? Why is this true?

1 Thessalonians 5:14
With whom should we be patient?

Ephesians 4:2
How does this passage describe patience?

Proverbs 19:11
What do we need in order to be patient?

1 Corinthians 13:4
What does this verse tell us about love?

Proverbs 14:29
What is the opposite of a patient man? How does he act?

James 5:7-8
Who is the example of patience in this passage? Why?

Ecclesiastes 7:8
Patience is better than what?

Romans 12:12
How should God's people act in times of hardship and trouble?

2 Peter 3:9, 15
Who shows patience in this passage? Why?

Proverbs 15:18
What can a patient man do? Why?

Galatians 5:22-23
This list is sometimes called the Fruit of the Spirit because people become more like Christ when God's Spirit lives in them. Does the Spirit help us have patience?

James 5:7-8
For what are we to wait patiently?

James 5:10-11
Who are the examples of patience in suffering we should follow?

Titus 2:13
For what are Christians waiting?

APPLICATION

It was Mark's turn to wash the supper dishes, but it was also the night of the big soccer game. Mark didn't want to be late for the game. In his hurry to get his work done, he broke the meat platter as he threw it into the sink.

God promised Abraham that he would have more descendants than he could count. As the years passed, Abraham and Sarah remained without a child, but Abraham believed God would do what He had promised. When Abraham was one hundred years old, Sarah gave birth to a son.

Donald asked his parents to buy him a pair of rollerblades. They told him they would pay him for doing work around the house so he could buy them himself. Donald knew it would take a couple of months to earn the money. He felt his parents were being unfair.

Esau came home tired and hungry after a day of hunting. When he asked for some stew that Jacob was making, Jacob offered to sell him some for Esau's special family position and inheritance. It was a high price to pay for a meal, but Esau agreed.

Joseph was put into Pharaoh's prison for a wrong he didn't do. While there, Joseph explained a dream that the king's cupbearer had. The cupbearer promised to speak to Pharaoh about Joseph, but he forgot. It took the cupbearer two long years to remember his promise and speak up for Joseph, who was then released from prison.

The swimming pool was crowded. Jan was eager to get to the diving board, but she walked carefully to the line at the board instead of hurrying. She knew it wasn't safe to run around a swimming pool.

The Israelite army and the Philistine army were ready to do battle. The prophet Samuel had told King Saul to wait for him to come and offer sacrifices to God before beginning the fight. Saul nervously waited until he couldn't stand it any longer. He offered the sacrifices himself, going against God's instructions, before Samuel arrived.

David, a shepherd boy, was chosen by God and anointed by the prophet Samuel to be the next king of Israel. But it was many years before David actually became king. During those years of waiting, David was a faithful citizen, obeying King Saul.

FIVE ALIVE!

by Susan Addington

TEACHING AIM: To review and reinforce any Bible story or lesson

MATERIALS NEEDED: A set of alphabet letter cards in a bag (the complete alphabet for each child)

PREPARATION: Print the alphabet on a large sheet of heavy paper and make a copy for each child. Cut out each letter and place them all in scrambled order in a paper bag.

PLAYING THE GAME: Each child picks ten letter cards from the bag and places them face down on the table. The "dealer" spells out a five-letter Bible word (from the story or lesson) on the chalkboard. Each child turns over one card. If it is one of the letters in the "dealer's" word, the child keeps it. Otherwise he discards it. Play continues until someone spells out the complete word.

NOTE: This game may be used with any Bible story or lesson that has five-letter words in it. For example, if you're teaching the Parable of the Sower and the Seeds, use words like these: grows, seeds, weeds, rocks, plant, roots.

Shining Star, Copyright © 1995

0-382-30651-1

BIBLE DOMINOES

by Joanne Wilson

TEACHING AIM: To help children learn and review the books of the New Testament

MATERIALS NEEDED: Construction paper (five different colors), black marker, books of the New Testament cut apart (below and pages 44-46), clear adhesive plastic (optional)

PREPARATION: Copy and cut apart the books of the New Testament on pages 44-46, including the New Testament book below. (Before cutting the pieces apart, you may want to cover the pages with clear adhesive plastic to make them more durable.) Cut out the five divisions of the New Testament, listed below from different colors of construction paper.

PLAYING THE GAME: Shuffle the book cards and give each child an even number. Children take turns laying their books to the right of the divisions they're in, but they must be put in correct order. (Example: If the first student has the book of Matthew, she may place it to the right of the GOSPELS division. However, if she has the book of Luke, she cannot play that card until the books of Matthew and Mark have been put down. The New Testament book may be used as a wild card, substituting for any book. The first child to play all his cards is the winner.

1 GOSPELS	2 HISTORY	3 PAUL'S LETTERS	4 OTHER LETTERS	5 PROPHECY

NEW TESTAMENT

Shining Star, Copyright © 1995

0-382-30651-1

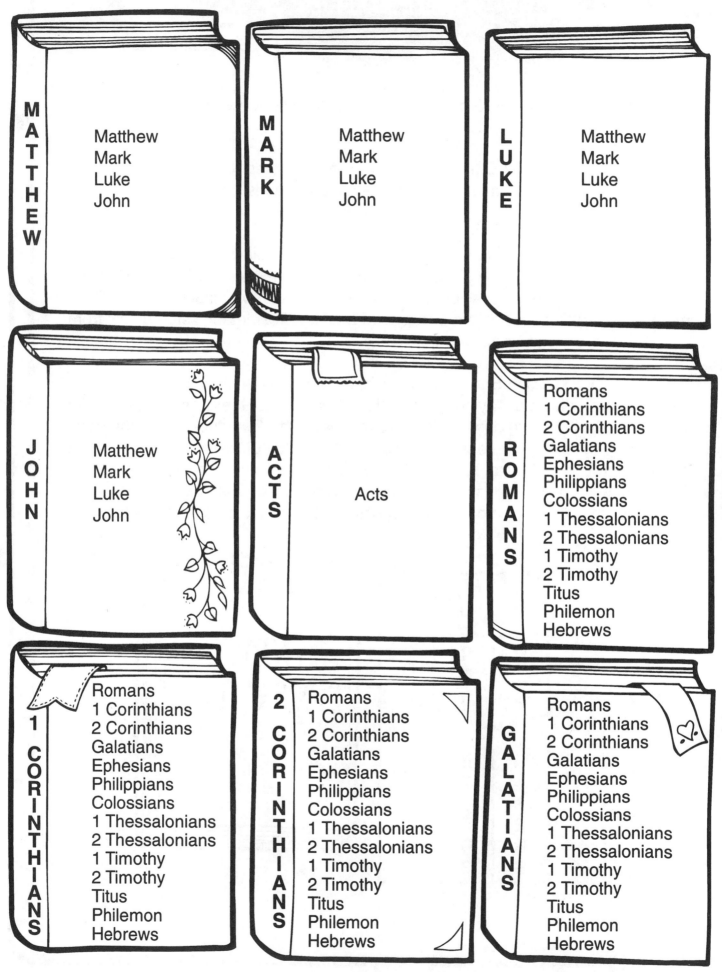

MATTHEW

Matthew
Mark
Luke
John

MARK

Matthew
Mark
Luke
John

LUKE

Matthew
Mark
Luke
John

JOHN

Matthew
Mark
Luke
John

ACTS

Acts

ROMANS

Romans
1 Corinthians
2 Corinthians
Galatians
Ephesians
Philippians
Colossians
1 Thessalonians
2 Thessalonians
1 Timothy
2 Timothy
Titus
Philemon
Hebrews

1 CORINTHIANS

Romans
1 Corinthians
2 Corinthians
Galatians
Ephesians
Philippians
Colossians
1 Thessalonians
2 Thessalonians
1 Timothy
2 Timothy
Titus
Philemon
Hebrews

2 CORINTHIANS

Romans
1 Corinthians
2 Corinthians
Galatians
Ephesians
Philippians
Colossians
1 Thessalonians
2 Thessalonians
1 Timothy
2 Timothy
Titus
Philemon
Hebrews

GALATIANS

Romans
1 Corinthians
2 Corinthians
Galatians
Ephesians
Philippians
Colossians
1 Thessalonians
2 Thessalonians
1 Timothy
2 Timothy
Titus
Philemon
Hebrews

Shining Star, Copyright © 1995

0-382-30651-1

EPHESIANS

Romans
1 Corinthians
2 Corinthians
Galatians
Ephesians
Philippians
Colossians
1 Thessalonians
2 Thessalonians
1 Timothy
2 Timothy
Titus
Philemon
Hebrews

PHILIPPIANS

Romans
1 Corinthians
2 Corinthians
Galatians
Ephesians
Philippians
Colossians
1 Thessalonians
2 Thessalonians
1 Timothy
2 Timothy
Titus
Philemon
Hebrews

COLOSSIANS

Romans
1 Corinthians
2 Corinthians
Galatians
Ephesians
Philippians
Colossians
1 Thessalonians
2 Thessalonians
1 Timothy
2 Timothy
Titus
Philemon
Hebrews

1 THESSALONIANS

Romans
1 Corinthians
2 Corinthians
Galatians
Ephesians
Philippians
Colossians
1 Thessalonians
2 Thessalonians
1 Timothy
2 Timothy
Titus
Philemon
Hebrews

2 THESSALONIANS

Romans
1 Corinthians
2 Corinthians
Galatians
Ephesians
Philippians
Colossians
1 Thessalonians
2 Thessalonians
1 Timothy
2 Timothy
Titus
Philemon
Hebrews

1 TIMOTHY

Romans
1 Corinthians
2 Corinthians
Galatians
Ephesians
Philippians
Colossians
1 Thessalonians
2 Thessalonians
1 Timothy
2 Timothy
Titus
Philemon
Hebrews

2 TIMOTHY

Romans
1 Corinthians
2 Corinthians
Galatians
Ephesians
Philippians
Colossians
1 Thessalonians
2 Thessalonians
1 Timothy
2 Timothy
Titus
Philemon
Hebrews

TITUS

Romans
1 Corinthians
2 Corinthians
Galatians
Ephesians
Philippians
Colossians
1 Thessalonians
2 Thessalonians
1 Timothy
2 Timothy
Titus
Philemon
Hebrews

PHILEMON

Romans
1 Corinthians
2 Corinthians
Galatians
Ephesians
Philippians
Colossians
1 Thessalonians
2 Thessalonians
1 Timothy
2 Timothy
Titus
Philemon
Hebrews

Shining Star, Copyright © 1995

0-382-30651-1

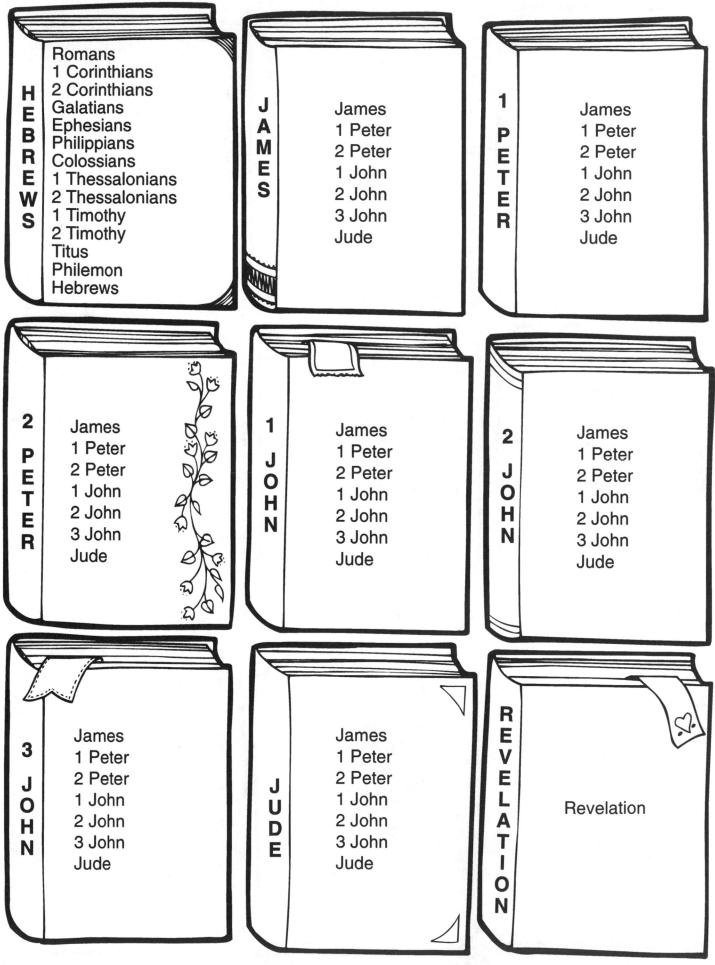

HEBREWS
Romans
1 Corinthians
2 Corinthians
Galatians
Ephesians
Philippians
Colossians
1 Thessalonians
2 Thessalonians
1 Timothy
2 Timothy
Titus
Philemon
Hebrews

JAMES
James
1 Peter
2 Peter
1 John
2 John
3 John
Jude

1 PETER
James
1 Peter
2 Peter
1 John
2 John
3 John
Jude

2 PETER
James
1 Peter
2 Peter
1 John
2 John
3 John
Jude

1 JOHN
James
1 Peter
2 Peter
1 John
2 John
3 John
Jude

2 JOHN
James
1 Peter
2 Peter
1 John
2 John
3 John
Jude

3 JOHN
James
1 Peter
2 Peter
1 John
2 John
3 John
Jude

JUDE
James
1 Peter
2 Peter
1 John
2 John
3 John
Jude

REVELATION
Revelation

Shining Star, Copyright © 1995

0-382-30651-1

THANKFULNESS MATCH-UP

by Mary Tucker

TEACHING AIM: To remind children of some of the blessings for which they need to thank God

MATERIALS NEEDED: Two copies of the match-up pictures on page 48, cut apart. (You may want to color the pictures with markers to make the game more attractive.)

PREPARATION: Put the two sets of match-up pictures face down on the table in scrambled order.

PLAYING THE GAME: Children take turns choosing two cards at a time and turning them over to try to match the pictures. When a child finds a match, he may keep the two pictures. The child with the most pictures at the end of the game is the winner. Take time to discuss the pictures and other blessings for which the children are thankful.

house	Bible	church	music
clothes	water	sunshine	brains
family	Jesus	trees	rain
food	pets	friends	flowers

Shining Star, Copyright © 1995

0-382-30651-1